P9-BZH-157

St. Helena Library

MORE MONOLOGUES
THEY HAVEN'T HEARD

Roger Karshner

Dramaline Publications
36-851 Palm View Road
Rancho Mirage, CA 92270
Phone 619/770-6076 Fax 619/770-4507

Cover Art, John Sabel

This book is printed on 55# Glatfelter acid-free paper, a paper that meets the requirements of the American Standard of Permanence of paper for printed library material.

CONTENTS

WOMEN: COMEDY

MAVIS

Mavis is displeased with her sports-obsessed boyfriend.

Sports, sports! It's all he ever thinks about, Darlene. Sports, sports, sports! He's a man possessed, I swear. I knew from the first he was into games, but I never suspected anything like this.

I should have suspected something on our first date when he insisted I come back to his apartment, and when we got there he showed me his collection of baseball trading cards. He keeps them in a fireproof safe along with a baseball fouled off by Pete Rose. He's just like a big kid. Like lots of guys are about sports. Once it gets in their blood—forget it.

Our time together is like this whirlwind of sports activity. Last weekend, we bowled on Friday night, took in a double-header on Saturday, on Sunday went to his company's softball beer bash, played miniature golf, and shot a fast game of pool. Then, Sunday evening, we watched a video of *Bull Durham*—twice!

Ron even has this Watchman TV he takes everywhere so he won't miss sporting events. The other night in a gourmet restaurant, he set the damned thing up right in the middle of Veal Oscar and started watching the fights and making side bets with the waiters. It was sickening trying to eat while watching some palooka with a nosebleed.

And he wears this greasy baseball cap all the time, too. Even with a pinstripe suit. And he eats Wheaties by the bale and talks about people with names like Nellie Fox. Have you ever heard of her?

The guy's totally flipped on sports—gone. And his obsession is really screwing up our relationship, too. He has a problem sexually because he's so damned preoccupied with sporting events. Ron may be bowling 250, Darlene, but in the bedroom he's throwing gutter-balls.

Never meddle with play-actors, for they're a favoured race.

Miguel de Cervantes (1547–1616)

CATHLEEN

Cathleen expresses her displeasure with the new clothing styles and the prices being asked for them.

Have you seen some of this stuff that their pushing as "new Fashion"? Who do these people think they're kidding here, anyhow? Name me one you know, any woman in her right mind would be caught dead in "The Baggy Look"? Okay, maybe for some fine-featured model who's seven feet tall and weighs eighty pounds it makes sense. But for the average person with a normal body—forget it! Every year these fashion gurus add some stupid new wrinkle, some new spin to sell women a load of unrealistic, overpriced junk. It's a joke, I'm telling you.

I don't know about you, honey, but I dress for men. I wanna keep them interested; want them to wonder about what's going on underneath, about the goodies, you know. Look, we may kid ourselves we're dressing for ourselves, but let's get real here, okay? We want to be attractive, alluring.

And show me one guy who's going to be turned on by some oversize fatigue outfit? Forget it. None. Unless he's got a thing for commandos in drag. The "Loose Look" is a loser unless you're overweight and want to cover up the fact that your favorite food is Snickers à la mode. And the same goes for "Active Wear." You think men don't know what's going on underneath sweats, that they don't know you're carrying around more blubber than a whaling ship.

And have you checked out the prices they're asking for some of these Paris tents? Five, six, seven-hundred dollars for Hefty bags. Ridiculous! Me? I'm sticking with the basics. Straight skirts, spiked heels, outfits that push me up and show me off and make men feel like having a feel.

If I'm such a legend, why am I so lonley?

Judy Garland (Frances Gumm, 1922–1969)

MARCIE

Marcie has recently joined a fitness club. Here she relates initial experiences, laments the rigors of shaping up.

Man, oh, man—do I ever ache! God, how I ache! And all over. Every muscle. Every little nook and cranny. I'm like this big, sore Thomas English Muffin. (*She stretches painfully.*) Ooooh! (*Feeling her soreness.*)

I don't know whether to laugh or cry. You know the feeling. Like when you get kicked in the shins. (*A pause for listening.*) When? I joined up just last week. For two-hundred seventy-five bucks. All the pain that money can buy. Then I laid out an arm and a leg for an outfit. You can't work out in these places unless you're hip. I'd got these cute, shocking-pink leotards, white tights, and yellow leg-warmers. And a hot pair of athletic shoes. The kind you can pump up. I tried the outfit on for Harold, and he said I looked like I was part of a mime troupe.

I had my first lesson yesterday. Murder. With about twenty other women of all shapes and sizes. The girl on one side of me just had to be anorexic. On the other side was this blimp stuffed into a lavender Spandex bodysuit. She looked like this jumbo, human sausage.

But some of the women looked fantastic. Like they should be in the diet cola commercials, you know. Big boobs, no waists, great legs, with butts like apples. And, oh yeah, you should have seen our instructress. Hey, you talk about built!

And energy! I've never seen anything like it in my life. This woman never stopped moving. Or smiling. Even when she put her head in her shoe, she was grinning like a door-to-door salesman. That's how flexible she was. No spine, Sally, I swear. She was a wet pretzel.

For aerobics, what they do is put on this real fast, super-loud disco-type music that you're supposed to do all this running and exercising to for thirty minutes. I started to fall apart after five.

I'm supposed to go back this Wednesday and get checked out on the Nautilus equipment. And then on Friday they said something about freeweights. What the hell's free about two-hundred seventy-five dollars? (*She moves painfully.*) Ouch! (*She moves her shoulders carefully while grimacing.*) You know what, Sally? I'll bet Jane Fonda's tendons are a mess.

I'm as pure as the driven slush.

Tallulah Bankhead (1902–1968)

FLORENCE

Florence tells how her relationship degenerated commensurate with her business success.

When I first started with IBM, Larry was all for it. That's when I was a secretary in the regional sales office. Back when I was typing, answering "heavy phones," bringing coffee—when I was an office slave.

But I saw the potentials. I saw what the outside sales guys were knocking down. These guys were doing all right. So, I decided to get into the sales end. I did a bunch of studying and kept after my boss, and finally they transferred me to the inside sales desk. When I told Larry, he thought it was okay but he wasn't really all that enthusiastic. His reaction was kind of like lukewarm, you might say. At best.

I did well on the sales desk, and within six months I was the top inside salesperson. And, little by little, I picked up bigger accounts. Which meant more commission, right?

I remember the night I told Larry how much I was making. He just grumbled and kept on reading his *Sports Illustrated*. With the new accounts, I was making as much as he was, so I offered to kick in more money towards the groceries and rent and stuff. Instead of being happy about it, he seemed to be pissed-off.

Then, last May, they gave me an outside territory, a good raise, expenses, and a company car. When I told Larry, he said

I was becoming obsessed with my job, and that I was becoming a cold and indifferent businessperson with masculine traits who was maybe a closet lesbian. The deal was, I'd become a threat, and the poor little baby couldn't handle the competition. His insecurity was showing. So long as I was what his mother had always been—a puppy dog who did household tricks—it was okay. But just let me start making it in the world, *his* world, and then, alluva sudden—then I was a cold, indifferent bitch.

So, Larry and I split up. He couldn't handle the idea of living with an equal. I understand he moved in with some mousey little thing who brings him his crown on a pillow every night. Tell me, Jan, how come so many men have their mentality between their legs?

If someone's dumb enough to offer me a million dollars to make a picture, I'm certainly not dumb enough to turn it down.

Elizabeth Taylor (1932–)

HANNA

Hanna, a nurse, talks of her beginnings.

At first—to be honest with you—I didn't think I'd make it.

You can study and intern and all of it, but let me tell you, there's nothing like on-the-job training—being there in the trenches, so to speak.

I thought my training had prepared me for the job. But the first few weeks were murder. Being around sickness constantly, seeing people die you've gotten attached to—hell, you form relationships. It's only human.

My first week, I had an older man on my floor who'd been operated on for prostate cancer. He had a tube in him and he kept groaning like crazy. Not that I blamed him. How would you feel with a tube up there? In some cases, we're lucky to be women.

I asked the head nurse to take me off his room. But she was about as understanding as your average IRS agent. And she was right. You can't go copping out. If you do, forget about nursing as a career and go into TV repair or something where the insides don't bleed. So, I faced up and hung in.

After a week, they took out the old fellow's tube, and he stopped groaning and looking so damned pitiful. It was evident he was feeling better. And I was feeling a lot better, too. Because I'd toughed it out.

The day the old fellow left—right before he was discharged—he said to me, he said, and I'll never forget it, "Hanna," he said, "I don't have a soul. No children. No family. Not even a close friend—nobody. But I want you to know that you've been like a daughter to me. Why, if it wasn't for you, I don't think I could have made it." And then he put his hand on mine and smiled, and I damned near cried. And then, right there and then, I knew why I'd decided to become a nurse.

It's better to be looked over than overlooked.

Mae West (1882–1980)

FRAN

Fran is a dipsy-doodle, off-the-wall pet freak. To paraphrase Will Rogers, "She never met an animal she didn't like."

Rabbits. They're so cute. All cuddly and soft. And nervous. You ever see a rabbit that wasn't nervous? It could be they're neurotic? I don't see why not. The poor little things. I have six: Harold, Albert, Don, Ida, Sally, and Frank. I like "people" names for my animals. Not stupid, whimsical names like Fluffy, Muffy, Cuddles—Spot.

I named my dog Weyerhaeuser. You know, after the tree people. I thought it sounded distinguished. And then, of course, there's dogwood. It all seemed to kind of like tie in, you know. And he's a German shepherd and Weyerhaeuser sounds German, don't you think?

I have four cats. All from the same litter. I knew the mother personally all through pregnancy and was there when her kittens were born. Just like Lamaze. I call them Eeney, Meeney, Miney, and Walter, because Moe reminds me of that dorky-looking guy in the Three Stooges. And besides, the Three Stooges made fun of animals in their routines. I can't stand people making fun of animals. They're so innocent. And sensitive. A person can't be too careful what he says around animals because they can be offended easily. Like my pet otter, Ron. He's extremely sensitive. But not nearly as sensitive as my parrot, Esther. She picks up on everything. You have to watch everything you say around her. And smart!? She knows all the Beatles' lyrics, the *Desiderata*, and a lot of Rod McKuen. Whatever happened to him? "A dog barked, I cut myself, and thought of you." Rod was one of the sixties' coolest guys. And I understand he loved pets. I read once in the *National Enquirer* where he had a couple sheepdogs he was living with in Malibu. If he likes animals, he's got to be all right. Lots of famous people are into animals. (*Noting her watch.*)

Wow! I'd like to hang around, but I gotta get home and feed my new rhesus monkey. He's still a bottle-baby. C'mon over sometime . . . we'll talk.

At one time I thought he wanted to be an actor. He had certain qualifications, including no money and a total lack of responsibility.

Hedda Hopper (1890–1966)

ANNIE

Annie and David are at variance regarding their relationship. David, motivated by jealousy, is pressing for marriage. Annie is content to perpetuate their live-in arrangement.

Look, as far as I'm concerned, things are okay like they are. I mean, we've been getting along great for three years like this, haven't we? So why go mess up a good thing? I've seen it happen time and time again. Here you have people living together who are getting along super, okay? Then they go and get married and everything goes to hell because now they feel locked in.

Anyway, I thought you were the one who was against rushing into marriage. And you know how I feel about it. Besides, we agreed, remember? (*A pause for listening.*) You've changed your mind. Well, I haven't changed mine. Marriage may be great for some people, but it's not for me. I'm just not the marrying type. At least not now, anyway. Neither of us are—not really.

I don't get it. (*She pauses for thought.*) Wait a minute, here! (*Pause.*) You're jealous! Yeah, that's it. Now I get the picture. It's because of that phone call I got from Steve, right? Right? (*A pause for response.*) Oh, yes it is. That's the deal. You're threatened. (*Pause for response.*) Like hell! That's it. Admit it. Just like a little kid with an old toy. You don't give a damn about it till someone else shows an interest. Then you want to lock it away in your attic. You talk about childish! (*A pause for listening.*)

C'mon, face it, you're being possessive. By getting married, nobody can have your toy and you'll be safe. Hell, Dave, there are no guarantees with marriage either. Can't you see that? If a person's going to mess around, they'll mess around. Anyway, Steve's certainly no problem. He's just lonely, that's all. Since Susan dumped him, he's going bananas. He's hurting.

The first thing guys do when they break up with someone is root through their memory bank of old girlfriends and start giving them a call. You know that. It's standard behavior. They hope there'll be a spark left over and they can get themselves a quickie for old time's sake.

Look, Dave, I couldn't care less about Steve or anybody else. You're it, okay? And I'm very happy. And I love you, and I don't want to alter a thing. Not right now, anyway. In time, if things work their way around to marriage—fine. But let's not push it just because somebody else wants to ride in your little red wagon.

I dress for women, and undress for men.

Angie Dickinson (1931–)

CONNIE

Connie doesn't mince words in telling of her distaste for astrology madness.

"What's your sign, baby?" How many times have you heard this one? Ten thousand, maybe?

What is it with all this astrology business, anyway? With these guys with their stars and their signs and their planets? Planets, hell! Their planets are in their pants. Face it, the whole sign thing is garbage. It's an opener, you know. A way of starting up a conversation they hope will lead to a Motel 6.

You know Mark, don't you? (*A pause for response.*) Sure you do. The big, good-looking blond guy who hangs out at Bailey's and drinks one draft beer all night. The guy who wears T-shirts and Go-aheads all the time. (*A pause for response.*) Yeah, that's him. Well, he's got this line where he asks every girl he meets if she's a Sag. Most of the time they say no. But every once in a while—due to the law of averages—he hits one who is, and she comes unglued because she thinks he's got psychic powers. The next thing she knows she's in Mark's apartment and he's out of his T-shirt and Go-aheads, with his Scorpio rising.

Remember Frank Goldberg? (*A pause for response.*) Sure you do. The creepy little guy with bad breath and food spots all over his clothes. (*A pause for response.*) That's him. Well, astrology was his thing, too. The guy must have read every book ever published on the subject. He was an authority, and he came across very scientific. He would look into your eyes intently and then he'd say, in this real low, mysterious voice, stuff like: "So, you were born on March fourteenth, huh? An important date. Albert Einstein was born on March fourteenth. You're an interesting combination with a creative imagination and you're caring, romantic, and affectionate. You're a mutable water sign, your color is sea green, your metal is tin." Then he'd rattle off some Shakespeare, toss in a little witchcraft, and a few rock lyrics. And, of course, the whole thing always came down to sex and how, because you were both water signs, you should get out of your clothes and take a shower together. And the sleazy little creep actually made out with this stuff, too. That's the disgusting part of it.

I don't know anything about any of it, and frankly I don't care. I don't know what my rising sign is or what house I was born in. Hey, I was born in a hospital.

All they ever did for me at MGM was change my leading men and the water in my pool.

Esther Williams (1923–)

MAXINE

Maxine, a no-nonsense woman, is savvy to the realities of the streets. Here she gives advice regarding the necessities of self-defense.

Tough? You bet I'm tough. You'd damned well better be in this day and age. It's survival out there, a regular jungle in the cities. These aren't like the days when you never locked your front door. Today you need alarms and bars and Dobermans and deadbolts up the ying-yang. This is how it is. This is today. This is reality.

I know this may sound paranoid, but I never take a shower anymore without looking behind the curtain first. For all you know, there could be another Norman Bates lurking around. Don't laugh. It happens. In case you haven't looked around, we're living in a violent society. Hey! A woman has to take precautions.

Last week over in Queens, a woman was raped right in church. What's this tell you? It tells you that you have to be careful about going into the confessional even, that's what. Is this a sad statement about what's going down in this country, or what?

This is the reason I got into karate. If some dude jumps this little lady—it's goodbye crotch. That's where you get 'em, you know—right in the business! (*She lifts her knee quickly to demonstrate.*) Or you go for the eyes! (*She slams her fingers forward in a gouging manner.*) Or you give 'em a quick spiked heel t' the ole shinbone. Or a car key to the eyeball. And you hit fast. You attack. You don't mess around. Not unless you wanna wind up nude somewhere over in Jersey.

You should get into karate. If you wanna continue to live in this neighborhood, you damned well better. Either that or get a gun and learn how to use it. Or move. But, even then, even in East Boondock you can still get hassled. Crime is on the rise all over the country. Hey, the papers are full of it.

My advice to women is to toughen up and be ready. And this doesn't mean you still can't be feminine. "Wear a garter belt and carry a big stick," that's my motto.

Romance on the High Seas *was Doris Day's first picture; that was before she became a virgin.*

Oscar Levant (1906–1972)

VALERIE

Valerie, a successful commercial writer, recalls her difficult and confused beginnings.

My dream was to become part of the Eastern literati. In the tradition of Cheever, Updike, and Styron. I wanted to capture their style, their usage of metaphor and symbolism. I wanted to write atmospheric stories about urbane men and women who didn't perspire when they make love. So, I studied their form and read all of their stuff and went to their lectures and got down everything they said on cassette. How witty they were, I thought, how entertainingly arcane and wry.

I tried to copy those guys. God knows, I tried. And it was murder. I would start a story, but by the second page I was out of gas. I'd get so damned frustrated and depressed I'd scream.

I wrote late at night and early in the morning before going to work. I lived it. And I was getting nowhere. And I was impossible to live with, too. I don't know how Jim put up with me because I was a grand pain in the ass carrying around a load of phony intellect. I thought in sepia and spoke in mauve and dressed like Miss Marple. I worked at being serious. I was so damned "heavy" in those days. Back then, the word *writer* was like the words *Pope* or *God*.

My first short story was a real upper about a suicidal poet. I submitted it with great expectations. It seemed like I got rejections the next day. I was crushed. I asked Jim what he honestly thought of the story, and he said the main character was about as charming as halitosis. When I broke down and bawled, he was consoling and understanding. He was wonderful. Then, he gave me some advice. I guess he thought I was ready to listen to something other than my cassettes of Cheever and Updike and Styron. He said that maybe I should forget about trying to write like those guys and write from the heart about things I knew. Like about pets and kids and the wacky, far-out types in our hometown.

So, I sat down and knocked out a short story about Olin Haverman, the town sheriff, who was also a meter-maid and a part-time counterman at the White Front Cafe. I sold it for three hundred dollars.

That was seven years ago. Since then, I've sold over thirty short stories and three novels. I'm currently working on a biography about a little girl who has polio and is very brave and wonderful. And, oh yes, today I work on a computer and no longer dress like Harriet Beecher Stowe.

As a young actress, I always had a rule.
If I didn't understand the line, I always
said it as though it were improper.

Dame Edith Evans (1888–1976)

WOMEN: DRAMA

MARGO

Margo speaks of women's rights and of ingrained masculine attitudes.

Please. Spare me. Okay? It's still, basically, a man's world, and you know it is. So far as a lot of men are concerned, women are second-class citizens, and they'd like to keep it this way.

A lot of men still relate to women as Mom or Sis or the little girl who needs to be "taken care of." With them, it's still the little-boy protective syndrome, and they continue to perpetuate it. It's part of their script. Basically, they're still little boys with this ingrained attitude who treat you like a sex object at work and in the bedroom. Face it, in many instances, this is still the case. (*Beat.*) Oh, my, I didn't mean to upset you! Relax, okay?

Why are you so threatened? I'm only stating a fact. There are still a lot of men out there who expect us to offer ourselves up like—like sacrifices, or something. To them, the words *woman* and *sex* are synonymous. I mean, sex is just taken for granted. It's as casual as a handshake to a lot of men. "Hello, my name's Ralph Gunther, in sales. You're cute. Let's rent a motel room." With some guys this is the attitude. And this is wrong. Sex isn't this casual, passing thing just because you're a man and I'm a woman.

I actually believe that some men still think we owe them sex; that it's our earthly duty to lie down and let them slobber over us like a girlie magazine. With some men it's still steak and rape. For a drink, a filet, and a little cheap wine, we're supposed to let them animalize us.

And a lot of women allow it, put up with this kind of behavior. Because a lot of women are locked into the old roles, the old attitudes. I think this upsets me even more than the sexist attitude of some men. Because, in this day and age, women should know the score, should be standing their ground and standing up and demanding respect both sexually and in the workplace.

And, little by little, women *are* gaining respect and job equality and better pay. Little by little, we're getting there. Little by little, women are realizing that they're suited for positions other than being spread-eagled on a mattress.

Scratch an actor and you'll find an actress.
Dorothy Parker (1893–1967)

CHRIS

Chris's mother's degenerating mental capacity necessitated placing her in a nursing home. Here, despite the practical necessity of the action, Chris expresses the natural contrition and regrets associated with parental confinement.

I was over there again yesterday. (*Beat.*) I didn't have any idea what it was like, not really. And Woodville seemed such a cheerful place when I checked it out, too. But—but with Mother in there, it's not cheerful at all. It's . . . hell, the whole thing's just plain tragic! (*A long pause. She squeezes her forehead as if attempting to cut off the recollection.*) But what could I do, Sandy? I couldn't keep her here any longer. Not like she was. Not in her condition. It was impossible to be with her every minute, and the expense of a full-time nurse was out of the question. (*She takes a photograph of her mother from a stand and examines it with an expression of deep melancholy.*)

Dear, sweet Mother. You were so beautiful, so lovely and giving. (*Looking up at Sandy.*) She was the last person on earth you'd think would get Alzheimer's. I guess there's just no way of knowing. (*Beat. She looks at the picture.*) To see her degenerate day after day, to watch her go downhill and become more helpless and disoriented and out of control. . . . (*Looking up from the photo.*) God! What's life all about, anyway? I'm glad Daddy isn't here to see it. I'd break his heart.

Woodville's the best home in the county but it's still depressing because it represents a place to spin out the rest of your days, a place to be put. "Put," Sandy. Think about it. Some day it could be you or me. Every time I think of her over there I. . . . (*A definite break. Then she regains her composure.*) At least there they'll be able to keep an eye on her. She wandered off twice, you know. The last time in her nightgown. And it was raining. I found her over in the park, staring at the children's swings.

You know, for a moment, standing there, she looked young again. I wonder if somehow, in that confused state of hers, she was remembering her childhood? It killed me to find her like that—soaking wet and bewildered.

She was always so proud of her appearance. (*Looking at the photograph.*) I just couldn't take the chance of her wandering off again. God only knows what could happen. So, I put her in Woodville Nursing Home. What else could I do, Sandy? What the hell else could I do?

The trouble with the rat race is that even if you win, you're still a rat.

Lily Tomlin (1939–)

JULIA

Julia warns an employee that any attempt at blackmail will prove personally disastrous.

You have a helluva lot of nerve, coming in here threatening me! You actually thought I'd be intimidated by somebody like you? (*A throaty laugh.*) Besides, who would believe you? The truth is a strange thing, Joe, it's as valid as who speaks it. And we all know what you are—a nobody! You're a nothing bastard who drifted into town and were lucky enough to get hired by my husband, who gave you a clean shirt and some respectability. And now you have "information" and we should pay you to keep quiet? (*Beat.*)

Sure we take kickbacks. Hell, yes. Sure we make deals. How about that? (*Beat.*)

So, you actually think you're going to bleed us because you have this kind of information, huh? Jesus, you're a joke. A pitiful goddamned joke! You're in way over your head, friend. You think we don't take precautions? (*A mocking laugh.*) Whose name do you think is on those papers? Mine? Dewey's? Hell, no, Joe—yours! (*A pause for his reaction.*) Yes, that's right—yours! Maybe in the future you'll be more careful about what you sign, my friend.

So, now who's in trouble, Joe boy? You so much as blab a word to anyone, and we'll bury you so damned deep they'll never find you. Bury you! Understand!?

I had you pegged from the first, you know. You with your phony charm and unctuous good looks. I know your type; I've seen plenty. Uneducated, basically crude, with enough con to get by. And you're a user, I spotted that right off, and I told Dewey. And there's only one way to treat a user—you *use* him.

Now, I want you to go back to your little office and do your little job for which you're grossly overpaid. Continue to act important and wear decent clothes and have lunches on the expense account. I won't mention anything about this to Dewey. We'll just keep it between the two of us, okay? But don't ever threaten again, ever. Because next time, Joe, honey—it's back to the gutter. Do I make myself perfectly clear?

I never thought of myself as pretty as a child, and I have tried to bring that awareness to my roles.

Jane Alexander (Jane Quigley 1939–)

LORRAINE

Lorraine, a former battered wife, tells of the violence triggered by an incident of infidelity and of lingering psychological scars.

I don't know why I did it. I was bored, I guess. Or maybe I needed to get caught. Who knows. (*A long pause.*)

I met Sam after work, and we started drinking, and one thing led to another. The next thing I know I'm loaded, and I wake up at one in the morning in his apartment. I called Karen and told her what had happened and asked her if Steve had called. When she said he hadn't, I asked her to cover for me. Then I called Steve and told him I was at Karen's, that I'd gotten drunk and decided to spend the night in the city at her place.

He never bought it. The next day, he inquired around and found out that I'd gotten smashed with Sam at Landsdale's. I knew he knew that evening. He didn't say anything, but he didn't have to, it was in his face. He had that sullen, cold look people get when they detest you. Then he came at me. It. . . . (*It's painful to recall.*) It was terrible.

It took fourteen stitches to close up my cheek. Afterwards, he was remorseful and guilty and tried to make it up to me. But it was over. Something like that ends it. And he knew it. But he still had the rage. He was still burning inside because he couldn't get it out of his mind about Sam.

The second time it happened, we were at the dinner table. It started with him questioning me about Sam, and then, alluva sudden, he jumped up and started beating me. He beat me until I passed out. When I woke up later in the hospital, they told me I had multiple contusions and a shattered jawbone. It was a nightmare. After I was released, I got a restraining order and moved upstate.

It's all over between us, but I'm still not the same. I can't stand the thought of a man touching me.

I'm working on the problem. I'm in therapy. And gradually, I'm coming around, becoming more trusting. Hopefully, one day soon, I'll be able to love again.

Imagination! Imagination! I put it first years ago, when I was asked what qualities I thought necessary for success upon the stage.

Ellen Terry (1847–1928), British actress

ELLEN

Ellen, a divorcee, admits to loneliness, tells of its debilitating effects, expresses her anxieties and fears.

It's been over two years since Kerry and I divorced. Too bad, but it was an impossible situation. Even though we had our moments, for the most part, we clashed. And he was so damned possessive. I felt hemmed in—suffocated.

But now, in a way, it's worse. Even though things weren't right between Kerry and me, at least then I wasn't. . . . (*An inner struggle against admission.*) Oh, Kay—I'm so damned lonely!

I wonder why it's so hard to admit? And to you, my best friend. It's just so damned hard to come out with. Hell, it'd be easier to admit to being strung out on drugs, or in debt, or. . . . But being lonely is so, I don't know—it's so ugly. It's something you carry around inside like this dirty little secret. You're afraid to tell people because, if you do, they'll peg you as a loser. And this is a catch-22. Because if you don't admit it, don't get it out in the open, it eats you up inside.

And I beat up on myself for what happened to my marriage, too. Even though it's no one's fault, I feel like I'm to blame. It's like I deserve to be lonely for screwing up. (*A beat for thought-gathering.*)

Last weekend was beautiful, remember? But not for me. For me it was hell. Because it seemed like all around me there were people with an "other"—with someone to share it with. It seemed like everybody in the world had someone but me. I came back here to the apartment and broke down and cried. I wanted to pick up the phone and call you right then, but. . . . Hell, I just couldn't. I needed a friend so badly, someone to unload on. But I was too embarrassed to call you on a Saturday night and admit I was scared and lonely and depressed.

It doesn't make sense, does it? I mean, I'm not old, not bad looking. But all the intellectualizing in the world doesn't help. I just can't seem to shake the loneliness and this nagging, overpowering feeling of low self-esteem. I need somebody. Somebody special. Somebody to fill the gap.

I've got to break out of this, Kay. If I don't, I'll go crazy.

(*Then, after a brief silence.*) I need your help. Help me, for crisesakes!

I stopped believing in Santa Claus at an early age. Mother took me to see him in a department store, and he asked for my autograph.

Shirley Temple (1928–)

MEN: COMEDY

FRED

Fred's weekend outings with girlfriend Lynda are leading to financial ruin. Here he describes a recent sojourn.

Forget it. I've got to cool it for a while. I'm broke, tapped-out. I spent a bundle on Lynda this weekend. A fucking fortune. I took her to a ballgame, then to dinner at some nouvelle-cuisine joint she loves where they get eighty bucks for strained food.

But what the hell can you do? I mean, Lynda's not the kind of woman you sit around the house with, you know. She wants to do things and be entertained and go places.

Like here a couple of weeks ago she insists we go to this bed and breakfast place way the hell out in the boonies. She'd read about in the travel section of the Sunday paper. So—off we go.

It was like checking into somebody's house, or something. It was weird. At first, to be honest, I was pissed. I mean, like who wants to live with some strange family and pay for it? Hell, we could have spent the weekend with my uncle, Carmine, for nothing. But once we got settled in, I gotta admit, it wasn't too bad. It was quaint, you know.

You should have seen the people who ran the joint. They were real cute and had faces like polished apples and looked like they'd been carved outta wood in the Black Forest. Hummel dolls. Lynda loved 'em. Especially the old man. She said I should take a lesson from him. How he didn't swear and didn't have to use profanity to make a point. I have to admit, the old guy was a real genteel motherfucker.

The place had only one bathroom for three couples. What a crock. I mean, we could have checked into a nice motel and had a john all to ourselves. But Lynda said that this was part of the charm of the place. Although I can't say I found standing in line with a bunch of dorks in the hallway very charming. But the breakfasts were great, I gotta give 'em that. Biscuits with gravy, and waffles with real maple syrup, and all kinds of homemade jams and jellies. Lynda insisted I buy a couple cases of their orange marmalade. Those bastards weren't quaint when it came to price, I'll tell you that, pal.

The breakfast was great, but the bed was terrible. It had a soft, lumpy mattress, and we kept rolling towards the middle all night long. And the worst part was, we couldn't make it because the springs squeaked, and Lynda said that other people would hear us and it would be embarrassing. Jesus! Forty bucks worth of marmalade and I didn't even get laid.

Cocaine is God's way of sayng you're making too much money.

Robin Williams (1951–)

SAM

Sam bemoans the tragedy of baldness.

Look, I don't wanna hear about it, okay? Anyway, with the ton of hair you've got, how would you know? It's always you guys with the mop of hair who give all the stupid advice.

You have got no idea what it's like to lose your hair. It affects you and makes you crazy. And all of the silly remarks about not being able to have hair and brains, too, and how bald is beautiful—that doesn't make it any easier. Look, if I had my choice, I'd trade what brains I have for a couple pounds of protein-rich, thick, wavy hair any day.

And all of the rationalizing in the world doesn't help, either. What it comes down to is most women don't go for chrome-domes. All this stuff about how baldness means virility and how the ladies gravitate toward bald-headed is the biggest scam since Nehru suits. Women don't dig baldies. Period! Not unless the guy's a millionaire. Then it's strictly for the bucks. You take away the money, they're outta there.

And there's nothing you can do about it, either. I know, because I've tried everything. Forget it. And transplants cost a fortune and usually come in strange and you wind up looking like a fucking jerk. And toupees are a joke. They never comb in right and they sit on your head like a dead muskrat. And the weave jobs and clip-ons and all that look awful, too; phony and lifeless and always a shade off in color. Like the stupid piece on the news guy on Channel 6. The sonofabitch looks like he's sitting under an orange bird's nest.

Frank, there's nothing redeeming about baldness—*nothing!* Thank your lucky fucking stars you look like Godzilla.

Actors should be treated like cattle.

Alfred Hitchcock (1889–1980)
Said in clarification of a remark attributed
to him, "Actors are like cattle."

JOHN

John attempts to convince his fiancée of the rationality of a prenuptial agreement.

Now, just a minute here, honey. Hold on just a sec. You're overreacting here. This has nothing to do with love. I mean— you know what I mean. It's got nothing to do with that. Of course we love each other, that's a given. But that's beside the point. I mean, sometimes things happen, you never know. I mean, nobody can predict the future. All I'm saying is that we should go into this thing weighing all the possibilities, looking at it from all angles. Do you realize that half the marriages in this country today end in divorce? We're talking half! Face it, this isn't a positive statistic. (*Pause for her response.*)

Okay, okay—I know how you feel; like how marriage should be old-fashioned, and all that. But that doesn't work anymore. It's not like we're living in 1750 on the frontier and I'll be skinning grizzlies and you'll be home baking cornbread. You're an executive and I'm a CPA, and we'll be living in Evanston in an expensive new condo with a trash compactor and a microwave. Look, all I'm saying is that we have a written agreement up front so that in case something happens, we're covered. It makes a helluva lot of sense. Think about it. Wouldn't you feel a lot better knowing that if something goes haywire, you could walk away without a big legal hassle, without having to overpay a couple of legal crooks to drag out something for months that should take no more than twenty minutes? Why pay some numb-nuts a fortune?

Look, in view of the divorce statistics, this is the rational thing to do. You wouldn't go out on the highway without some kind of insurance, would you? Hell, of course not. So—so look at this as marriage insurance, okay?

I'll tell you what. Don't think of me as your future husband right now, okay? Put passion aside for a minute and take a cold, hard look at the bottom line. (*He smiles nervously.*)

Whaddaya say—partner?

When I played drunks, I had to remain sober because I didn't know how to play them when I was drunk.

Richard Burton (Richard Jenkins, 1925–1984)

FRANK

Frank, a country feller, graphically relates his cousin Ray's fatal addiction to motorcycles.

Ray lived on that there motorsickle all that summer. Tearin' 'round like some crazy man. He took m' brother Bob fer a ride on it out on 422 one day, an' Bob said he had that thing t' up over a hundred an' that it was a-shakin' like a dog on ice. When 'e got off, 'e swore t' never git back on one a them things again. An' Bob's a daredevil!

We all tried our best t' talk t' Ray. We tole 'im 'e was gonna wind up a-wrappin' that there bike around a pole some day. But 'e wouldn't listen. Then it happened:

It was on a Sunday, I 'member. Aunt Ida an' Uncle Ory was over. And it was hotter 'n hell. We was all settin' out under the arbor tryin' t' keep cool. We was eatin' some a George Drum's homemade ice cream. Strawberry, I think it was. We was settin' there a-talkin' hog prices when we hear this here explosion. Shook the whole valley, it did. Uncle Ory said that after the sermon he'd heard that morning, he thought it was the end a the world fer sure. It sure sounded like it.

Well, what happened is ole Ray had come up over a little rise out on Kingston Pike a-goin' better 'n ninety, an' on the other side a that rise, Estil Pritchard was a-comin' with a truckload a nitro. Understand that that there motorsickle took off a that there rise a-flyin' an' smacked headlong inta the bed a that there truck.

Neither Ray er Estil knew what hit 'em. Killed both of 'em outright. An' the impact a the explosion blew ole Ray right outta 'is shoes. They found 'em later 'bout a quarter-mile away in the top a Earle Dressback's barn. Two-tones, I think they was. There wasn't enough left a them boys t' stuff a turkey with. Sheriff an' 'is deputies picked up the pieces in a Mason jar.

Was one helluva note.

All tragedies are finish'd by a death,
All comedies are ended by a marriage.

Lord Byron (1788–1824)

GIL

Gil, a smooth operator with the girls, draws an analogy between baseball and women.

The way I have it figured, making out is a lot like baseball. The only difference is, when you come up to bat against most woman, you've already got two strikes on you and the pitcher you're facing never throws balls. That's the reason you have to get a hit on your first swing.

Now, most guys just aren't ready for the majors. Most are minor-leaguers. And women know this. They can sense it. They know that they're Nolan Ryan and you're Humpty Dumpty from Podunk.

(*Pointing.*) Take that lady over there, for instance. The blonde in the corner booth with the tight pants and the sexy red shoes. That, gentlemen, is a twenty-game winner if I ever saw one. You go up against her without preparation and she'll blow you away. You come at her with something up and over the plate, like, "Can I buy you a drink, honey?" and you're outta the game, back in the dugout with an ice-pack on your tongue.

It's all a great big ballgame, pure and simple. And with great- looking women, it's always the seventh game of the Series and you're at the plate in the bottom of the ninth with a man in scoring position. And you're facing a flame thrower on the mound. It's the big moment in the Fall Classic. And do you get a hit, or do you choke? Got the picture? Do you get suckered on a slider or crunch one into the gap? (*He places his beer on the table, rises, straightens himself.*)

Well, guys, I'm up. So, watch me and maybe you clowns'll learn something. Keep an eye on a three-hundred hitter. I mean, like, boys—get ready for a grand slam. (*He fairly glides across the room.*)

The bad end unhappily, the good unluckily.
That is what tragedy means.

Tom Stoppard (1937–)

HAROLD

Harold's girlfriend is an upwardly mobile computer technician who is married to her profession. Here, Harold levels with her, informs her of her obsession with her work and how it may lead to alienation.

Dammit, Kelly, you're just not getting the point here. It's not that I don't have respect for your work, it's just that you've become obsessed with it, that's all.

Talking to you anymore is like taking a course at Cal Tech, do you realize that? And you never let up. Lately you never give it a rest. Look, it's great to be interested in your work. I understand this. I'm interested in my work, too. I like the retail clothing business. But I don't sit around all night putting people to sleep with how we mark down socks. And in my business we use common terms. We say, *coat* and *pants* and *Jockey shorts*. At least people can focus on what we're talking about without taking a course at MIT.

Like tonight at dinner with Teri and Dave. You did an hour and a half on bytes and kilobytes and megabytes to the point where nobody could take a bite. And c'mon—how many people are intensely interested in how a central-processing unit is wired?

I don't mean to be overly critical here. So, please don't get the wrong idea. I really respect you for your intelligence and for working yourself up like you have, I really do. You've got brains and know-how, and on top of it all, you're beautiful. But in all honesty, Kelly, it's time you face up to the fact you've become a high-tech pain in the ass.

I know you don't want to hear this, but it's high time somebody said something. You're great and sweet and people respect you. And I love you. But you've got to back off with the high-tech buzzwords and constantly talking about your job. If you don't, pretty soon the only audience you're going to have is you.

As an actor, I have no desire for anybody to understand my past work. Period.

Jack Nicholson (1937–   )

IRV

After a long-awaited assignation, Irv expresses frustration with Ruth's reluctance to participate.

I know we're married, Ruth. I know this, you think I don't know this? Big deal. Like this is a first here, or something? Like this hasn't ever been done before in the entire history of man- and womankind. Just in case you haven't heard, this has been going on for a long time, Ruth. And it's not a crime. They don't arrest you for being unfaithful.

This wasn't a solo idea, Ruth, remember that. This was your idea, too. In fact, you instigated it. You said, "Irv," I distinctly remember you saying, "Irv, we have an attraction and have had ever since we danced the hora at the Langbaum wedding on that beautiful day when it alluva sudden rained and turned my dress into a wet T-shirt." I remember you saying this as plain as day. Then we make plans. We talk. For over six months, we talk. We talk on phones. We talk at the garage between lube jobs. We talk in whispers behind Sally's and Dave's backs and giggle because it's dangerous and risky and we think it's cute.

And then we make a plan. It's all agreed. And we make up stories and I get this room and we check in under the name of Mister and Missus Harry Clark of New Rochelle. This was all planned at great time and expense and trouble.

And now we're here and alluva sudden it's cold feet because we're maried. Of course we're married! So, what! What else is new? We knew this from the first and discussed it, and you said being married made it more exciting. And now, guilt.

Ruth, this is no time for feeling guilty. We can be guilty later. This is time for getting undressed. So, let's make the best of it. Look, Ruth, we're just normal, faithful, married people who want to see somebody else naked before we die.

The reason why Absurdist plays take place in No Man's Land with only two characters is primarily financial.

Arthur Adamov (1908–1970), Russian-born French dramatist

JACK

Jack, an aspiring actor, speaks of his job as a bartender, his theatrical ambitions, a current stage project.

Yep, you've got it, all right. You see and hear it all on this job. I could write a book. Maybe someday I will.

Everyone who walks in here is a story. See that guy down there at the end of the bar? The little guy with the cheap cigar? He's a retired schoolteacher. He comes in here every evening about seven and closes the place up. He taught manual training in junior high. You'll notice he has a finger missing. All manual- training teachers have a finger missing.

Yeah, we get all kinds. The place is a real zoo, let me tell you. But it's a pretty quiet bar because the management doesn't stand for any rough stuff. The guy who owns the place is Italian and he has "friends," if you know what I mean. If somebody gets out of line, he makes a call, and in a few minutes a guy shows up who casts shadows. His name is Aldo and he has hands like King Kong. What he does is put his fingers over your head and start squeezing. After a couple of seconds, whoever's causing a problem gets the hell out—fast. Either that, or he winds up with a permanent headache. (*A pause for listening.*)

Me? I'm an actor. I'm just doing this part-time till I get a break. I'm doing a play now. A musical by a couple of young writers called *Dirty Tricks*. It's about the Watergate thing. It has good music and a good book and the band is heavy-metal. I play the lead. It's a helluva part. A rock 'n' roll Nixon.

We already have some big people interested. If they come up with enough money, we'll be able to move the show to a bigger theatre. In that case, I'm outta here. I won't be mixing drinks anymore. I'll be busy polishing up my Richard Milhaus. He's a tough study. Playing a guy who knows he's lying and doesn't show it ain't easy.

Some of my plays pan out, and some peter out.

J. M. Barrie (1860–1937), British novelist and dramatist

CLARK

Clark, an executive dropout, finds solace in eschewing the business life.

"What's a guy like me doing selling live bait in a backwater place like this?" Hey, I've been asked the question a hundred times. And a hundred times I've said that I'm here because I had a taste of the so-called executive life, and they can have it.

After I graduated from Ohio State, I took a job in Cincinnati with Procter & Gamble. I was part of their marketing team. I worked on such wondrous items as Joy and Bold and Tide and products with monosyllabic names. I was involved in these interminable, inane meetings where we'd argue about what color we should use on a box of new detergent, for instance. They were all-day sessions and we wouldn't break for lunch. We'd send out for pizza and cold cuts.

I was part of the team for over four years. I had the ball and I was running with it. And I was scared as hell of dropping it. Heaven forbid you drop the ball. They paid me two-hundred thousand dollars a year and perks to scrutinize printouts, analyze consumer questionnaires, and determine how we should move in the marketplace. *Marketplace.* Don't you just love that term? After about five years, I began to develop gastric problems. At first, I thought it was the pizza and cold cuts diet. No way. What I was experiencing was stress due to executive overload. I was suffering from one of the most common diseases known to modern culture—Corporate Cancer!

So, early one Monday morning, I walk into my supervisor's office and tell him to take his two-hundred thousand and perks and introduce it to his lower intestine. Then I moved here and bought this live-bait store, and now my only gastronomical problems are severe withdrawal symptoms when I don't get enough junk food. And I love it here. I love the people and I love my bait. A wonderful group of night crawlers, grub worms, and crayfish that never posture, talk on cellular phones, or give a shit about the colors on the new Tide box. It's great being part of their team.

Tragedy is if I cut my finger. Comedy is if I walk into an open sewer and die.

Mel Brooks (Melvyn Kaminsky, 1926–   )

ARNIE

Arnie, in a burst of oversimplification, enumerates the pitfalls attendant to the sexual revolution.

No, I'm not kidding. Ask Randy; he was there. She came over and hit on me. Boom! Just like that. (*He sucks on his beer.*)

That's what's happening today, this is what's going down. A lot of women today come on; they're up front. It's part of the movement, being liberated and all that. Things have really turned around. (*He sips and reflects.*)

Remember Jane? You know, the little blonde with the big hooters who drives the white Mustang? Same thing. Me and Tom are over at the Sundance having a beer, and she comes over wearing this white tank top full of pink nipples and asks me to dance. It's crazy today, babe. (*He takes a thoughtful glub of brew.*)

The way I look at it, if a girl hits on me, then how many other guys, you know. Ten—a hundred? Who needs this? You know how much disease and stuff is around today? There's no way in the world I'm taking that kind of chance. No way. (*Sips. Another thoughtful pause.*)

You'd think this'd be the greatest time for a guy, too. With women so open, and everything. But you have to be super careful today. It's to the point where I want health certificates and X-rays—current. Either that or I go with her while they run some tests.

You remember Jason Lymon III? You know, the nice-looking dude from Hillsborough who always wore a suit and suede shoes? (*Pause.*) Well, he goes and picks up some stuff you wouldn't believe. Stuff that shots don't phase. I understand there's a strain going around you can't blow out with TNT. Well, anyway, Lymon finally winds up in the hospital with mono and his folks find out. Wow. How about having to tell your mother? (*He shudders at the thought, takes another drink.*)

I think the safest way to have a relationship today is to be introduced by a friend or take out someone you know real well. And then—then you use fifty layers of protection. Hell, but even then you can't be sure. (*Deep thought.*)

Do you know what? We've gone and liberated ourselves right back to rubbers.

---

*If I had my career aagain? Maybe
I'd say to myself, Speed up a little.*

James Stewart (1908–)

MEN: DRAMA

JOE

Joe, due to drunken recklessness, is responsible for the death of the woman he loved. In this speech, he reflects contrition and also expresses bitterness for events that he feels contributed to the tragic incident.

I shoulda known better than t' go over there that day. People should always know when what they do is stupid and wasteful. But sometimes we don't, do we? Nope, sometimes, even when we know there's not a damn bit of sense to it, we go too far. I guess that's just the way it is with us creatures.

And I'd been drinkin' all that morning. Somethin' I should never do. 'Specially when things are wearin' on me. 'Cause liquor at a time like that is somethin' a guy like me hides behind and uses as an excuse to do what he knows he shouldn't. (*Beat.*)

Yeah, I shoulda stayed away for sure. Maybe it's 'cause Cyrus told me I couldn't come, maybe that's the reason. There ain't nothin' like takin' a thing away from a person to make him want it all the more.

I loved Martha an' just couldn't stand the thought of never seein' 'er again. When the old man said I couldn't, I went crazy; all fuzzy an' outta control; rollin' downhill without any brakes on me. Joe Ives just wasn't good enough for his daughter. I was good enough for a friend, to work for 'im, but someone like *me* wasn't good enough for his flesh and blood.

He had no right t' try an' keep us apart. No right, goddammit! So, I just couldn't stay away. I just couldn't help myself, that's all. I've never ever felt so much hurt. Inside I was empty, like someone had turned me over and poured me out. I was sick and angry and in love. In love with the only thing in the world that meant a damn to me, something that alluva sudden I had taken away. And ya know why? 'Cause I wasn't good enough—'cause I hadn't gone to the right schools—'cause I didn't measure up—'cause I was "different." Hell, alluva sudden I wasn't part of the human race. I was nothin' but a *thing*. But a thing with feelings—that's what he forgot.

Chaplin is no business man—all he knows is that he can't take anything less.

Samuel Goldwyn (Samuel Goldfish, 1882–1974)

DEWEY

Dewey, a hard-knocking, self-made man, speaks with great fervor against the environmental restrictions placed upon industry and of their often-devastating effects.

The point is, this town's been healthy for years because a Barnes' Manufacturing! This little snot-pile of a burg owes its existence to it! So, we cut a corner here and there. Big fucking deal. Who the hell doesn't?

Nobody ever gave a good goddamn about a little waste being dumped here and there. Not till we got a handful of so-called enlightened people in this county who didn't know shit from Shinola and made a big deal and stuck their noses in and make it damn near impossible for us to operate! Sure, I could have installed the cleanup crap, sure. And it would of cost a fortune and would of put a plant the size of mine right outta business! I wonder how half the town would have felt about being out of work?

Nobody complained except a few liberal, politically correct, self-righteous sonsabitches, anyway. Nobody. The local merchants? Are you kidding? The city council? Never! They all knew if we had to meet all of the stupid requirements, we'd be finished and so would they. And they were right. Right because they know the world keeps turning and that they have to get up in the morning and make a living and face the hard realities. And you can't please everybody and bend over backwards and give in to every goddamn stupid whim.

All of this purity crap's for the textbooks. For assholes like you, Brad, who think life's a white shirt that never gets mussed! If it wasn't for guys like me, guys who busted their balls and started on shoestrings and worked and sweated and stayed with it, it would all come to a grinding halt. You may question my ethics—okay, fine. That's your privilege.

I'll tell ya what—you go out and take a vote. Go out and ask the people of this town if they want ethics or wanna eat! Go on, ask 'em—college boy.

Farce is the essential theatre. Farce refined becomes high comedy: farce brutalized becomes tragedy.

Gordon Craig (1872–1966), British actor

STICKS

Sticks, a jazz musician, is effusive in his expression of anger and frustration regarding the current state of things.

Oh, yeah? Are you kidding? People are still going outta their gourds. Serbs knocking off people right and left. Iraq still controlled by some fucking Arab John Wayne. And how about Africa? Crazy-ass tribes playing human safari. And rebel bastards starving people to death in third world countries. And the thing with the Jews and the Palestine cats. And how about these smaller countries run by macho-tyrants who are busy making bombs in their basements? Every little guy on the block wants the big marbles so he can kick ass and become a hero and get his face in the history books. And there's the jerk-offs willing to use germ warfare, and terror, and . . . you name it. And don't go forgetting Latin America—a regular hot tamale. And Korea.

Believe me, the world could still go, baby. And what about the crazies running around the streets? The cities are screwed. Rape, murder, car-jackings, gangs—you name it. And the whole mess is being orchestrated by the news guys, the million-dollar news readers in funny clothes with negative, basset hound faces—media terrorists. And people in general, the way they treat each other. Like shit. What's the last time someone opened a door for you, huh? And when they did, you looked back to see if you still hand you wallet.

And then, there's the government with its laws in your bedroom, and its hands on your paycheck. Hey, that there's terror, too, man—the worst kind—'cause you could come home some night and find a US Senator busting open your piggy bank. You can't trust the people in charge. Show me a person who says he's honest, and I'll show you a person with a motive. All the major cats are into power and control, man. Political cats devote their entire lives to pulling the little guy's dick.

I like to play the line and not wander too far to either side. If a guy has just had a bad day in the mines and wants to see a good shoot-'em-up, that's great.

Clint Eastwood (1930–   )

BARNEY

Barney, an ex-boxer, speaks with a slur as a result of too many punches. He tells of his rise and fall, his alcoholism, his drug dependency, and psychological problems stemming from an abusive, possessive father.

From the time I was a little kid, my old man pushed me to be a fighter. He always told me it was all I was fit for. He always did that, ya know, put me down.

The old man was dead set on me being a boxer. He showed me what he knew and took me to bars where I shadow boxed so he could bet booze money. Later he got me a decent trainer, and I won the Junior Golden Gloves and turned pro at 18. I was good and fast and flashy and a crowd-pleaser. I finally got a shot at the title—which I won. I was the youngest champion in my division, ever.

I had money, girls—everything. I was on top. But I was a mess. I got married to a nice girl, but I blew it. I hung out and was unfaithful and I started drinking and doing drugs. I won some big fights for big purses, but after three years I had nothing and *was* nothing. After three years at the top, I was a nobody. My wife left me and took my daughter, and I was broke and nobody would have anything to do with me anymore. I had a few more fights but kept sinking lower until, finally, I was a drugged-out bum living on the streets, grubbing for food like an animal. And my dad, he wouldn't have anything to do with me, wouldn't speak to me even.

I was on the bottom when I met Shirley, a friend of my old manager's. She got me into AA and into thinking about what made me tick. Now I see things.

Ya know what? I never even wanted to be a boxer in the first place. That was my dad. He wanted me to be what he couldn't because he was a drunk and a failure and he could be somebody through me.

Looking back on it now, I know that I never ever fought a fight for myself. Not really. Hell, I fought to please my old man. I was fighting for him, so maybe he would love me.

I'll just go on playing Rambo and Rocky. Both are money-making machines that can't be switched off.

Sylvester Stallone (1946–)

STEWART

Stewart, a young, terminal AIDS patient, unloads his anger.

Yes, I'm bitter! And why shouldn't I be? How would you feel? How would you like to give it up, all of this—your life? Christ, I haven't even lived. (*He turns away for a few seconds.*) Death is something that happens to other people, not you. You don't consider it; it's out of the question, an abstract thing.

I don't want to die! I don't want to leave you and the sky, the trees—people. You think about all of this, you know. You think about how it'll be without you around and how things will be still going on like always and how you're not going to be part of it. That's one of the tragedies of it. You're gone and you're nothing but an occasional memory or an old photo in a shoebox in someone's closet.

You know you're not the first to die. You know this, and it makes sense. And you know there's nothing you can do, anyway. You repeat this logic to yourself over and over, try to sell yourself. But you don't buy it.

Right now, I don't know if I'll be able to face death with dignity or not. Right now I'm afraid. And I'm damned mad!

ORDER DIRECT

MONOLOGUES THEY HAVEN'T HEARD, Karshner. Speeches for men and women. $9.95.
MORE MONOLOGUES HAVEN'T HEARD, Karshner. More living-language speeches. $9.95.
FOR WOMEN: MONOLOGUES THEY HAVEN'T HEARD, Pomerance. $8.95.
MONOLOGUES for KIDS, Roddy. 28 wonderful speeches for boys and girls. $8.95.
MORE MONOLOGUES for KIDS, Roddy. More great speeches for boys and girls. $8.95.
SCENES for KIDS, Roddy. 30 scenes for girls and boys. $8.95.
MONOLOGUES for TEENAGERS, Karshner. Contemporary teen speeches. $9.95.
SCENES for TEENAGERS, Karshner. Scenes for today's teen boys and girls. $9.95.
HIGH-SCHOOL MONOLOGUES THEY HAVEN'T HEARD, Karshner. $8.95.
MONOLOGUES from the CLASSICS, ed. Karshner. $8.95.
SHAKESPEARE'S MONOLOGUES THEY HAVEN'T HEARD, ed. Dotterer. $8.95.
MONOLOGUES from CHEKHOV, trans. Cartwright. $8.95.
MONOLOGUES from GEORGE BERNARD SHAW, ed. Michaels. $7.95.
MONOLOGUES from OSCAR WILDE, ed. Michaels. $7.95.
WOMAN, Pomerance. Monologues for actresses. $8.95.
MODERN SCENES for WOMEN, Pomerance. Scenes for today's actresses. $7.95.
MONOLOGUES from MOLIERE, trans. Dotterer. $9.95.
SHAKESPEARE'S MONOLOGUES for WOMEN, ed. Dotterer. $8.95.
DIALECT MONOLOGUES, Karshner/Stern. 13 essential dialects applied to contemporary monologues. Book and cassette tape. $19.95.
YOU SAID a MOUTHFUL, Karshner. Tongue twisters galore. $8.95.
TEENAGE MOUTH, Karshner. Modern monologues for young men and women. $8.95.
SHAKESPEARE'S LADIES, ed. Dotterer. $7.95.
BETH HENLEY: MONOLOGUES for WOMEN, Henley. *Crimes of the Heart*, others. $8.95.
CITY WOMEN, Smith. 20 powerful, urban monologues. Great audition pieces. $7.95.
KIDS' STUFF, Roddy. 30 great audition pieces for children. $9.95.
KNAVES, KNIGHTS, and KINGS, ed. Dotterer. Shakespeare's speeches for men. $8.95.
DIALECT MONOLOGUES, VOL. II, Karshner/Stern. 14 more important dialects. Farsi, Afrikaans, Asian Indian, etc. Book and cassette tape. $19.95.
RED LICORICE, Tippit. 31 great scene-monologues for preteens. $8.95.
MODERN MONOLOGUES for MODERN KIDS, Mauro. $8.95.
A WOMAN SPEAKS: WOMEN FAMOUS, INFAMOUS and UNKNOWN, ed. Cosentino. $9.95.
FITTING IN. Monologues for kids, Mauro. $8.95.
VOICES. Speeches from writings of famous women, ed. Cosentino. $9.95.
FOR WOMEN: MORE MONOLOGUES THEY HAVEN'T HEARD, Pomerance. $8.95.
NEIL SIMON MONOLOGUES. From the plays of America's foremost playwright. $12.95.
CLASSIC MOUTH, ed. Cosentino. Speeches for kids from famous literature. $8.95.
POCKET MONOLOGUES for WOMEN, Pomerance. 30 modern speeches. $9.95.
WHEN KIDS ACHIEVE, Mauro. Positive monologues for preteen boys and girls. $8.95.
FOR WOMEN: POCKET MONOLOGUES from SHAKESPEARE, Dotterer. $8.95
MONOLOGUES for TEENAGE GIRLS, Pomerance. $8.95.
POCKET MONOLOGUES for MEN, Karshner. $8.95.
COLD READING and HOW to BE GOOD at IT. Hoffman. $9.95.
POCKET MONOLOGUES: WORKING-CLASS CHARACTERS FOR WOMEN, Pomerance. $8.95.
MORE MONOLOGUES FOR TEENAGERS, Karshner. $8.95.